LONDON MIDLAND
STEAM ON SHED

LNER STEAM

MORE GREAT WESTERN
STEAM IN DEVON

SOUTHERN
STEAM IN ACTION

SOUTHERN WORKS STEAM

BORDER STEAM

LIGHT RAILWAYS
standard gauge and narrow gauge
OF BRITAIN

ARTICULATED LOCOMOTIVES
OF THE WORLD

MAIN LINE STEAM

STEAM IN india

SCOTTISH RAILWAYS
in the heyday of steam

GREAT WESTERN
STEAM THROUGH THE YEARS

WESTERNS

SUPERPOWER STEAM
AROUND THE WORLD

BRITISH TRAMS

SCOTTISH
BRANCH LINE
STEAM

THE MIDLAND RAILWAY

the later years of

GREAT WESTERN

LMSR LOCOMOTIVES

BR STANDARD STEAM in close-up

80037

BR STANDARD STEAM IN CLOSE-UP

edited by

TONY FAIRCLOUGH AND ALAN WILLS

D. BRADFORD BARTON LIMITED

Frontispiece: Standard Class '4' 2-6-4T No.80037 accelerates away from Evercreech Junction on the Somerset & Dorset line with the 4.20 p.m. Templecombe to Bath on 31 July 1965. [Hugh Ballantyne]

IRRC 2975/4N *ISBN 0 85153 346 9*

printed in Great Britain by Whitstable Litho Ltd., Whitstable, Kent
and bound by The Newdigate Press Ltd., Dorking for the publishers

D. BRADFORD BARTON LTD · Trethellan House · Truro · Cornwall · England

A Standard in all its glory: No.73051 in immaculate condition at Eastleigh, 4 July 1965. [L. Elsey]

introduction

Over the years, many locomotive classes have aroused controversy, but never before has a whole series of designs been surrounded by dissent, yet such has been the fate of the Standard classes which were built by British Railways in the early years of Nationalisation. The main element of the argument has always been 'Why were they ever built in the first place?' and it may be said that, apart from the Class '9' 2-10-0s, there were locomotive classes of equal ability to the eventual Standard designs already available on the constituent Regions of BR, which could have fulfilled the operating department's requirements until the demise of steam. There were some commentators who believed that no more steam power should have been built at all and that available resources should have been allocated to the development of newer forms of motive power, while there were those who saw in the new machines the dead hand of governmental interference at work through the state-owned transport set-up. However, following Nationalisation in January 1948 it was decided by the newly-formed Railway Executive that because of the economic climate, steam would have to continue as the mainstay for some years to come and that it would be politic to develop new locomotives which were not too obviously based upon any of the original 'Big Four' types, as this would have smacked of favouritism and been the source of possible friction between the Regions.

In the new organisation the cult of personality was not allowed to assume too large a proportion as had happened in the old companies, where such Chief Mechanical Engineers as Churchward, Gresley, Stanier and Bulleid imposed their ideas firmly upon the departments under their control. The man given responsibility for Mechanical and Electrical Engineering on the Railway Executive was Robin A. Riddles who had spent many years on the LNWR and LMSR, becoming Principal Assistant to Stanier and finally Chief Stores Superintendent, besides designing the 'Austerity' freight locomotives during the Second World War. Under the overall command of Riddles were two officers closely concerned with locomotive affairs; Roland C.

Bond of the former LMSR became Chief Officer (Loco Construction and Maintenance) and E.S. Cox (ex-LYR and LMSR) was appointed Executive Officer (Design). The latter was ultimately responsible to Riddles but in practice was given the remit of producing designs for the new range of Standard locomotives and rolling stock. So, as is the usual custom, while the Standards are referred to as 'Riddles locomotives', they were largely the brain children of Cox and his team, formed of the chief draughtsmen of the old 'Company' drawing offices. These men—J.W. Caldwell from Derby, E. Windle of Doncaster, F.C. Mattingly the long serving Swindon man, and C.S. Cocks from Brighton, with R.G. Jarvis, ex-Derby and latterly of Brighton joining later—formed a group which brought their collective experience together in the production of the new designs. However, with the top posts going exclusively to ex-LMSR men it was obvious that the influence of that Company was bound to predominate and in some quarters this caused bitter comment and resentment. Fortunately the men of the design team (the Chief Draughtsman's Committee) worked well together, putting aside old loyalties and using their vast experience for the benefit of the new concern. Detailed design work was allocated to the Regional Drawing Offices, with Derby made responsible for Pacifics and the Class '2's, Doncaster the Class '5' 4-6-0 and the Class '4' Mogul, Swindon the Class '3's and Brighton having the Class '4' 4-6-0 and 2-6-4T plus the big Class '9' 2-10-0. Each office was also allotted special components, Derby having such items as wheels, tenders and associated equipment, Doncaster the cylinders, motion and valve gear, Brighton the brake gear, and Swindon the boilers. The mainstream of all this activity was under the close control of E.S. Cox who regularly visited the Regional offices, while Riddles overlooked the whole and made the final decisions.

The basic ethos of the new designs was simplicity of construction and operation. Two cylinders were the general rule, the solitary Class '8' being the exception, with every effort made to ease the work of preparation and disposal at the running sheds by the use of self-cleaning smokeboxes, hopper ash pans, drop grates, mechanical lubricators and similar modern aids. Outside cylinders and Walschaerts valve gear helped the accessibility. In order to meet the problems of poor post-war fuel and lower standards of firing skills, the engines had large firegrates and were made as simple as possible to operate. All of this was most commendable, being largely based on North American practice, but many regretted that the opportunity was not taken of making the final phase of British steam development follow the paths blazed by the great French engineers with the use of full compounding and other intricacies, even though the times were against such ideals. Had the economic conditions of the 1950s been different then perhaps the complexities of such as the Bulleid Pacifics might usefully have been incorporated into the Standard range, but with labour scarce and expensive, ease of maintenance and operation had to have priority. A further aim was to have the widest range of operation throughout the system and the engines were designed to either the L1 or L2 loading gauges. The former covered most of the lines of British Railways while the latter restricted the larger locomotives to the principal main line routes.

As may be imagined, the appearance of the first Standard the Class '7' Pacific, was eagerly awaited, albeit with some trepidation. To locomen used to engines based upon years of steady development on their old railways, the prospect of entirely new machines was none too welcome. When the 'Britannias' first appeared, with their high running plates, exposed wheels and cluttered-looking tenders, many of their worst initial fears were realised, although things did not appear to be as bad as with the Ivatt engines of the LMSR which had come from almost the same stable. Perhaps the tragedy of the Standards has been that the criticisms so often levelled at the various classes have been based largely upon preconceived prejudices for, in the main, the locomotives performed the duties for which they were designed with economy and at moderate maintenance costs. While it is not the purpose of the present volume to assess the performance of these locomotives in day-to-day service, it may be said that the reception accorded to individual classes varied in relation to the types of locomotive which they replaced or supplemented. For example, Great Eastern section men took to the 'Britannias' as being superior to their previous 'B1' 4-6-0s, while the Southern men found that Class '5' 4-6-0s responded in a similar way to the popular 'King Arthurs' and made a welcome change from the idiosyncrasies of the Bulleid 'West Countries'. Yet on the Western Region the 'Britannias' were put alongside 'Kings' and 'Castles' and found wanting, while ex-LMS and LNE men preferred their own types for the heaviest duties. In retrospect it would seem that the smaller Standards generally proved more popular than the larger types as they replaced worn out mixed-traffics on intermediate turns in various parts of Britain. Then of course there were the magnificent 2-10-0s which broke entirely new ground in Britain and proved to be one of the greatest of British classes, bringing much credit to all concerned with their design and construction. Perhaps the Standards would have been received with greater favour if they had been built by one of the former companies, (especially the LMSR) as they would have had the backing of the built-in loyalty which was an integral part of our old railway system. Thought of in that light, the Standards were undoubtedly a fine series of engines.

Six of the twelve designs have been included in this volume, namely the Class '7' 4-6-2, Class '6' 4-6-2, Class '5' 4-6-0, Class '4' 2-6-0, Class '4' 2-6-4T and Class '3' 2-6-2T. The remaining classes will feature in a subsequent companion volume.

Throughout the history of railways, most locomotive engineers have wanted to start their careers with a successful express design, and the Nationalised team were no exception. The first Standard locomotive to appear was the pioneer Class '7' 4-6-2 No.70000 *Britannia* which, while nominally a mixed-traffic, was in reality a fully-fledged express design, having 6ft. 2in. coupled wheels and a modern front-end, which enabled her to exceed 90 m.p.h. in service without any difficulty. This head-on view of No.70004 *William Shakespeare* at Stewarts Lane on 2 April 1955 displays one of the surprise features of the new family of engines, namely a deep fall plate between the smokebox and the buffer beam, an item which was partially relieved by the deflectors on the Pacifics.
[Brian Morrison]

The evening sun of 23 August 1956 highlights No.70004 *William Shakespeare* at Eastleigh. This engine, together with No.70014 *Iron Duke,* spent her early years at Stewarts Lane shed, where she was excellently maintained for use on the 'Golden Arrow'. This particular member of the class had received an exhibition finish before she was displayed on the South Bank site of the Festival of Britain in 1951, which helped to give an added fillip to 'the Lane's' cleaners. It will be readily apparent that the copper pipes and other

bright work have been burnished and the Brunswick green paintwork well oiled over, thus making the very best of the Standard's functional good looks. Of all the unfamiliar features displayed by these new engines, it was probably the high running plates which first struck a jarring note to the eye, yet in time, these became acceptable. [L. Elsey]

70004
WILLIAM SHAKESPEARE
40

70004
WILLIAM SHAKESPEARE
40

On 8 August 1954, No.70004 *William Shakespeare,* the pride of Stewarts Lane shed, was given a trial run on one of the Western Section's heavy boat trains from Waterloo to Southampton Docks. Here we see the Pacific easing off railway property to cross Canute Road into the Old Docks. *Below:* a few minutes later, however, the Immortal Bard has come to grief on the sharply curved track at the entrance to No.1 shed. The 94-ton engine is leaning against the platform and this adventure marked the class's first and last appearance in the Old Docks. [L. Elsey]

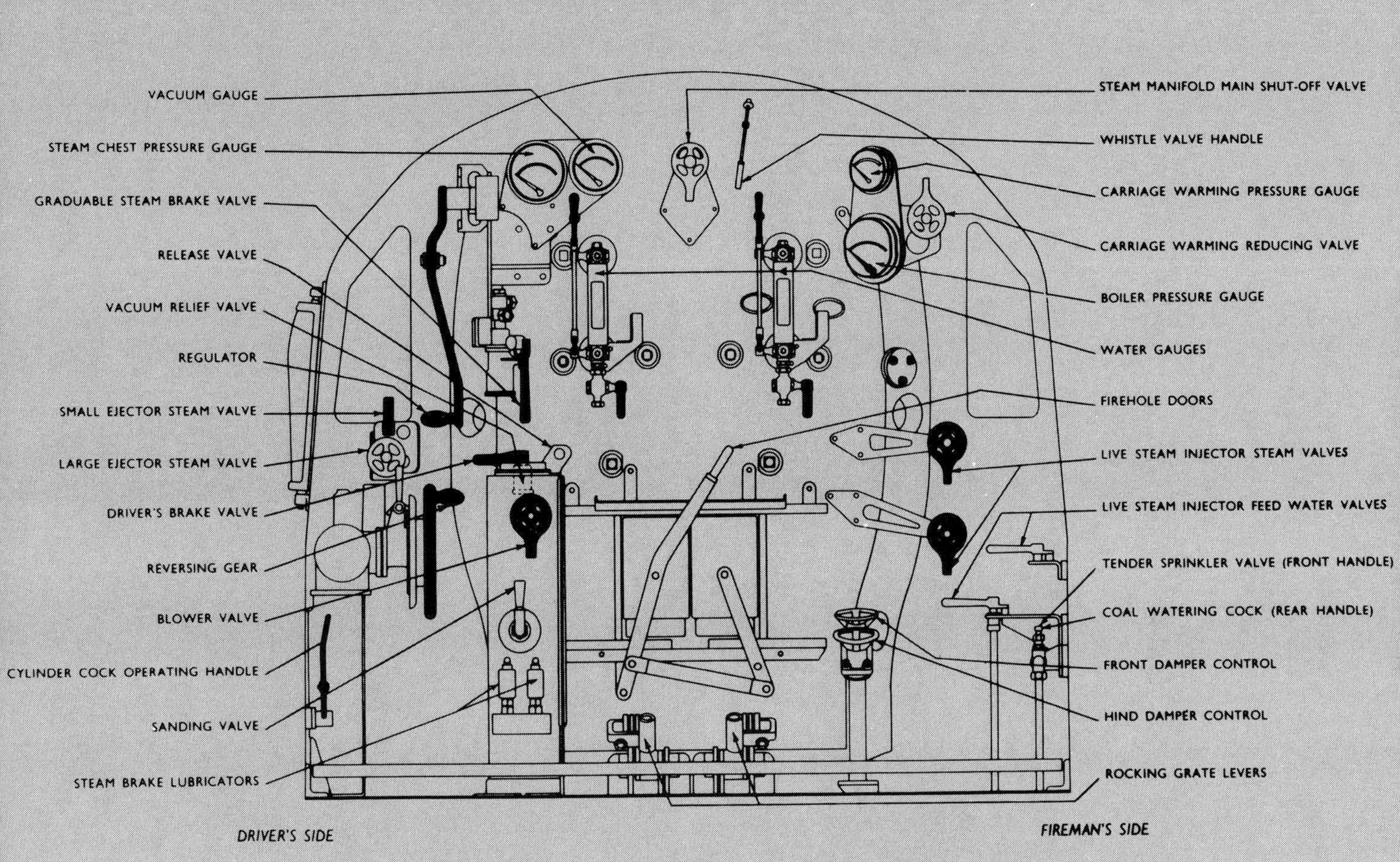

Much thought had been given to the footplate layout of the new Standards. A wooden mock-up had first been produced, which had been inspected (and criticised) by enginemen who were to work on the new machines. Most (but not the Western men) approved of the new arrangements. The pull-out regulator handle and the grouping of driver's controls to the left and fireman's to the right of the cab is reminiscent of Bulleid's Southern practice. [Alan Wills Collection]

CORNISH
RIVIERA
70019
LIGHTNING

One of the smaller 'Britannia' nameplates, that of No.70046 *Anzac,* (photographed at Rugby, 6 July 1960). Cast in brass, with raised 4in. lettering, these plates had either a red or black background and were bolted to the smoke deflectors. The names were varied in character, ranging from famous literary and historical figures through traditional ex-GWR names to Scottish firths, while one, No.70047 remained nameless throughout her career. [M. J. Jackson]

A 'Britannia', No.70019 *Lightning* of Laira shed, in that most Western and westerly setting of Penzance on 26 April 1952. These Laira-based Pacifics were the biggest engines ever to work into Cornwall and their 20¼-ton axle loading must have been near the limit for the Royal Albert Bridge at Saltash. As a regular performer on Western Region. No.70019 has been fitted with GWR-type automatic train control, the contact shoe being visible between the front bogie wheels. It will be noticed that the front steam-heating flexible pipe has been removed for storage during the summer months. [Brian A. Butt]

A cab-side close-up of No.70013 *Oliver Cromwell* in Lostock Hall shed yard near Preston, on 4 August 1968. When the 'Britannias' first appeared, there was considerable criticism of the shortened cab sheets, the levels of which did not match the lower limits of the tender sides, but this was deliberate design policy which allowed easy access to fittings and equipment below the footplate. The first thirty-five Pacifics were equipped with Timken roller bearings on all axles, these being expensive in first costs but giving the promise of long and trouble-free service. The live steam injector can be seen immediately in front of the pony truck, while the vacuum ejector is mounted on the firebox immediately in front of the cab.
[Hugh Ballantyne]

A youthful enthusiast proudly surveys the scene from the fireman's seat of No.70014 *Iron Duke* at Eastleigh, 10 July 1951. Bottom right, in front of the trailing truck is the Davies & Metcalfe Class 'K' exhaust steam injector with its delivery pipe rising vertically from the cone before turning at right angles towards the clack valve at the front of the boiler. Above the injector is the rod controlling the front damper, behind which is a large washout connector. Above the trailing truck is the separate water valve which controls the flow of water from the tender to the injector. Live steam arrives at the injector through the front upper pipe and the exhaust steam passes into the front of the injector. Above the running plate are two steam valves, the upper for the exhaust and the lower for the live steam injectors. The highest valve on the firebox side controls the flow of steam for carriage heating. [L. Elsey]

By 18 September 1967, when this view of No.70014 was taken at Carnforth, the original *Iron Duke* nameplates had been removed for safe keeping but otherwise there has been little modification of the 'Britannia' design. The smokebox is of the circular type fixed to a saddle with its domed door secured by a central dart. Inside are the self-cleaning screens which deflect ash through the chimney; this apparatus would keep the box clear of ash for upwards of a fortnight. Much thought had been given to the design of the blast pipe and chimney, but finally, following a great deal of research by S.O. Ell at Swindon, a simple but critically measured single chimney and blast pipe was adopted for the Class '7' Pacifics. [M.J. Jackson]

No.70013 *Oliver Cromwell* at Carnforth on Guy Fawkes Day, 1967. In order to give the drivers fine control over the steam supply it was decided to use a superheater multi-valve regulator in the header of the Pacifics. This required external rodding while access to the regulator valves was obtained by removing the raised plate which is visible behind the chimney. The cylinder cocks were steam operated.
[M.J. Jackson]

70016
ARIEL
86C SC
70016

One of Western Region's Class '7's, No.70016 *Ariel,* of Cardiff Canton (86C) shed, at Hereford with a parcels train on 5 May 1960. This engine betrays a Western feature—the removal of the handrails on the smoke deflectors and the substitution of six hand holds. This modification followed the derailment at speed of No.70026 near Didcot in 1955 when it was alleged that the hand rails had impaired the driver's vision. [M.J. Jackson]

The final batch of 'Britannias', Nos.70045-54, were turned out in 1954 and were paired with a modified design of tender. This was the BR 1D which carried 9 tons of coal and was equipped with a steam pusher. Earlier members of the class had been tried on the Holyhead-Euston boat trains, when the 7-ton tender capacity had proved insufficient, but these latest engines proved masters of the job and were popular with their crews. However, No.70045 (formerly *Lord Rowallan)* had migrated north and is seen at Kingmoor, Carlisle, on 11 August 1966. [M.J. Jackson]

No.70012 (ex *John of Gaunt*), seen at Carnforth on 15 October 1967, was one of the original batch of 'Britannias' which were built with a cantilevered footplate. In theory, the fixing of the cab structure to the boiler instead of the frames should have produced a very firm base for the crew but unfortunately the design, which lacked a fall plate between the engine and tender, plus the 'stepped in' contour of the tender itself led to the setting up of severe draughts and swirling eddies around the rear of the cab. Canvas screens between the cab and tender were provided in an attempt to alleviate this problem. [M.J. Jackson]

The doyen of all the Standards, No.70000 *Britannia* at an unusual location, Ash, on 4 October 1964, at the head of an LCGB special to Portsmouth and the Isle of Wight. No doubt the famous engine had been specially requested for this duty, but she looks to be in poor shape for a prestige turn. The original 'Britannias' coupling rods were fluted but in later years many were fitted with plain section rods. The battery box for the recently-fitted AWS equipment may be seen on the running plate above the large diameter exhaust steam pipe leading to the injector. [A.R. Butcher]

No.70049 *Solway Firth* on 29 October 1967 at Carnforth. [M. J. Jackson]

No.70046 *Anzac* at Kingmoor, 2 September 1966. In order to obtain further performance data, Nos.70040-9 had plain boxes on all coupled wheels, while Nos.70035-9 had roller bearings on the driving wheels only. In general service, little difference could be distinguished between the variations, a tribute to the great improvements in plain bearing design and manufacture which had occurred in the post-war years. [M.J. Jackson]

Pacifics Nos. 70054 *Dornoch Forth* and 70006 *Robert Burns* on Kingmoor shed, 2 September 1966. [M.J. Jackson]

Partially dismantled No. 70020 *Mercury* at Upperby shed, 2 September 1966. It was the original intention to 'go American' and build the engine with bar frames but because of maintenance problems in BR workshops it was decided to retain the traditional British plate frames. On the 'Britannias', 1¼in. thick plates were used, with a 2in. thick extension riveted to the rear end for the drag box. The faces of the axle boxes in contact with the horn guides had manganese steel liners welded on to the box to reduce wear and maintenance costs. [M.J. Jackson]

The 'Britannias', like all the Standards, were equipped with wide running plates but access from the front was made difficult by the narrow section alongside the smoke deflectors. The revolving reversing shaft may be seen in this view of No.70013 *Oliver Cromwell* at Bressingham in August 1978. The cord for the tri-tone whistle runs through the right-hand boiler rail. [C.E. Dann]

The Class '7's had valves and cylinders lubricated by atomised oil supplied through mechanical lubricators driven by pumps actuated from the valve gear via the round-section rods seen on No.70013. Originally the atomisers came into action when the regulator was opened, the driver having an indication of the oil pressure by means of a gauge in the cab. When coasting the regulator should be slightly opened to supply atomised oil to the front end (as in GWR practice) but men from other Regions found the custom strange and usually coasted with the regulator shut. As a result, in later engines, the atomiser valve was connected to the cylinder cock controls which, when shut, opened the atomiser. The three-piece slide bars, used for the larger Standards designed to clear the L2 loading gauge, were derived from Gresley's LNER practice and enabled a lightweight crosshead to be fitted. The 20in. x 28in. cylinders were of cast steel with cast iron liners and box-type pistons.
[C.E. Dann]

The GWR type of live steam injector was adopted for the Standards. The steam passes down the upper right-hand pipe, with the water inlet situated below. Water is forced by the steam through the combining cone in the main barrel of the injector and out through the delivery cone and pipe seen on the left of the photograph.
[C.E. Dann]

The 6ft.2in. coupled wheels of the 'Britannias' were of traditional British aspect, although Bulleid's idea of shrinking the tyre on to the wheel centre without other means of fastening was adopted. Much of the pipework was tastefully hidden beneath the running plates. No.70013, Bressingham 1978. [C.E. Dann]

Close-up detail of No.70013's big end and return crank. The Walschaerts valve gear actuated piston valves having the large diameter of 11in. and a travel of 7¾in. in the full forward gear of 78%. The travel at 20% was as much as 4in. and with a steam lap of $1\frac{11}{16}$in. it was ensured that these Class '7's could be run economically on short cut-offs, thus using the expansive powers of the steam to the full. [C.E. Dann]

The Class '6' 4-6-2s, introduced in 1951, were built following the success of the Bulleid 'West Country' concept. With an axle loading of 18½ tons and a tractive effort of 27,520 lbs, the design provided high power possibilities for the majority of the country's lines. In many respects these engines were scaled down 'Britannias', having an identical chassis, but with a smaller boiler and slightly smaller cylinders (19½in. x 28in.). The working pressure of 225 lb/sq.in. was 25 lbs. less than that of the larger Pacifics which had a tractive effort of 32,150 lbs. The 'Clans' had roller bearings on all axles and had similar fittings and accessories to the 'Britannias'. No.72006, *Clan Mackenzie* of Kingmoor (12A) shed stands at Greskine signal box, halfway down Beattock bank, awaiting clearance into the next up block section on 11 October 1963.

[Hugh Ballantyne]

72006
CLAN MACKENZIE

No.72005 *Clan Macgregor* outside the paint shop at Crewe Works in July 1956. Like the other Pacifics, the 'Clans' were allocated to the Derby design office, but built at Crewe and most of the repair and heavy maintenance work was carried out at the ex-LNWR headquarters. [M.J. Jackson]

The 'Clans' were coupled to the BR 1 type of tender which weighed 47 tons, holding 7 tons of coal and 4250 gallons of water. The inset coal bunker was successful in providing a good view when running tender-first but unfortunately when running normally it set up severe draughts which caused coal dust to swirl around. (And how often did large Pacifics run tender-first, anyway?). No.72007 *Clan MacKintosh* is seen at Carlisle on 16 August 1966. [L. Elsey]

).72001 *Clan Cameron* at Polmadie shed in Glasgow, alongside No.70054 *Dornoch* ·*rth,* 27 June 1957. The comparative sizes of the boilers show up in this view, the :.4in. minimum of the 'Clan' contrasting with the 5ft.9in. at the front end of the ass '7'. Bogies and pony trucks of the two Pacific classes were interchangeable. [Brian Morrison]

As befitted engines which were to spend all their life working in Scotland or on its borders, the Class '6's bore the splendid names of Scottish clans. Unfortunately only ten were built as it was found that the class of work for which they had been designed could be performed equally well by the 'Britannias' or the smaller Class '5' 4-6-0s and so these light Pacifics remained something of an enigma. They rarely appeared on the more famous routes on which amateur train timers abounded and hence they received scant publicity, but among the Scottish enginemen who handled them on the difficult routes in south-west Scotland they were quite popular, and that was praise indeed for such men were among the most expert in Britain and not easily satisfied. The cast brass nameplates of *Clan Campbell* (No.72002) and *Clan Buchanan* (No.72000) had raised 4in. letters and were very similar to those of the other Standard Pacifics. Names which have not appeared in this volume were *Clan Fraser* (No.72003), *MacDonald* (No.72004). *MacLeod* (No.72008) *Stewart* (No.72009). If only the class had multiplied what a fine array of names we might have had.

[Brian Morrison]

By 18 February 1966 when this view of No.72006 (*Clan MacKenzie*) was taken at Ayr, the first five 'Clans', Nos.72000-4 of Polmadie shed had already gone to the scrap heap, and this one looks in a most woebegone condition. It seems wrong that such up-to-date machinery as the Standard engines should have been written off after so short a career, but higher authority had decreed that steam must go and even modern units such as this were sadly neglected in these latter years of steam working. If a more gradual and orderly phasing-out had occurred as on the Continent, these engines would have had another dozen years or so of active service to their credit. [Derek Cross]

For service in the Class 5 power range, it was first suggested that a small 4-6-2 would be ideal, but the problems of first cost and increased maintenance charges were weighed against the fact that a very successful Class 5 already existed in great numbers. This latter was of course the Stanier 4-6-0 of which over 800 had been built. Hence final thinking decided in favour of a 'Standardised' Stanier 4-6-0, the 73xxx being the result. As this view of No.73009 at Perth in August 1951 shows, the new 4-6-0 design looked very much one of the new Standard family of engines, with its high running plates and deep fall plate beneath the smokebox, a feature which gave rise to their early nickname of 'Town Halls'. [M.J. Jackson]

No.73025, of Cardiff Canton (86C) shed, at Burton-on-Trent on 28 August 1955. The BR 3 type boiler was very similar in general dimensions to the Stanier Class '5' one having 225 lbs./sq.in. working pressure and outside diameters of 4ft.11$\frac{11}{16}$in.–5ft.8½in. This well-proven steam raiser was further improved in later years after scientific testing revealed that by decreasing the blast pipe diameter from 5⅛in. to 4⅞in. a 26 per cent increase in steam production could result. [Brian Morrison]

The Class '5's first appeared with the same type of tri-tone hooter as supplied to the Pacifics but unusually mounted immediately behind the chimney on the 4-6-0s. Later members of the class had a traditional British whistle mounted in front of the cab. No.73001 has arrived at Swindon and prepared for a visit to the Factory for overhaul, 10 February 1960. The cabs of these early 4-6-0s were fixed to the boilers, with the footplate extended by cantilever to the tender as on the Pacifics. [M.J. Jackson]

No.73049, one of the Somerset & Dorset line's popular stud of Class '5's, at Eastleigh on 11 December 1955. The first fifty engines were coupled to BR 1 type tenders which had a capacity of 4250 gallons of water and 7 tons of coal, but there were several variants of tender attached to later engines in the class. The majority had lined black livery as seen in this view. [L. Elsey]

A cabside view of No.73051, ex-works at Eastleigh on 4 July 1965. The Class '5's were fitted with Davies & Metcalfe Class K exhaust steam injectors on the right hand side with a separate water valve situated above. The ex-GWR type live steam injector is also on the right hand side of the locomotive hidden behind the exhaust injector. This green painted 4-6-0 has a modified cab as may be seen by the absence of the second full length grab rail on the cab side sheets; note the rail in place on the tender which has the traditional fall plate. The general arrangement of the tender front is visible, with its open coal door, shovelling plate and tender handbrake handle. [L. Elsey]

The 'other end' of No.73051 showing the Walschaerts valve gear, which was interchangeable with that on the Classes '6' and '7' Pacifics. Lubrication of the cylinders and valves was by means of atomised oil supplied through mechanical lubricators driven from the valve gear, while the motion was lubricated by grease supplied by hand or power gun at the running sheds. The bogie was also standard with those on the Pacifics, having 3ft. diameter carrying wheels. Behind the coupled wheels are the bearing springs which were built up with eighteen 5in. by ½in. carbon steel plates having a maximum span of 4ft. [L. Elsey]
Below: diagram of Walschaerts valve gear. [Alan Wills Collection]

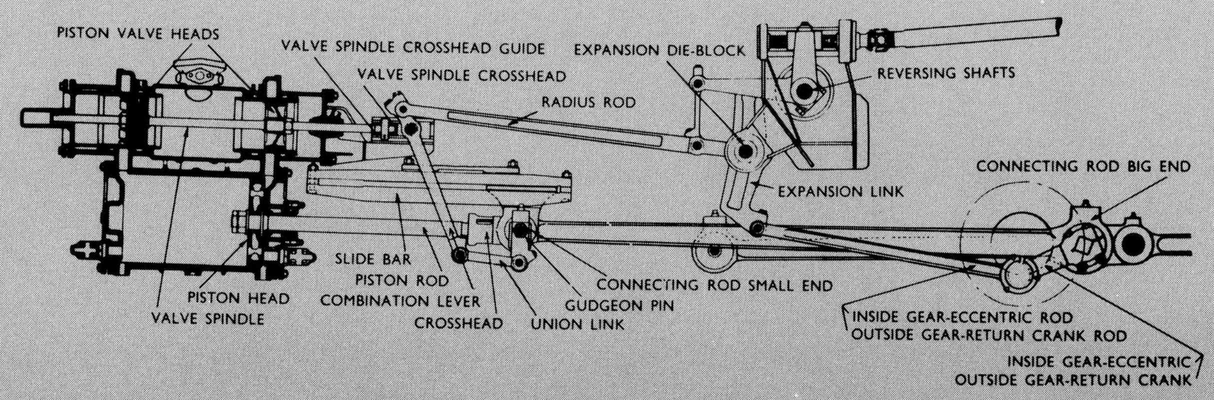

Several varieties of tender were attached to the Class '5's to meet the varied needs of each region. The Southern's main problem was water supply as there were no water troughs available. The type illustrated here (BR 1B) had a coal capacity of 7 tons and could take 4725 gallons of water which was adequate for the majority of the Southern's longest non-stop runs. The flush-side tenders proved more popular with the men than the original inset models, while the normal fall-plate again pleased the crews. Generous locker space was provided at the front of the tender above the shovelling plate. It will be noted that the coal space has been shortened: more coal than the 7-ton capacity could have been accommodated but this might have resulted in a certain amount remaining unburnt at the back of the bunker for a long period, this leading to deterioration in quality. *Right:* a close-up of the same tender, taken on 12 January 1959, showing the axle boxes with their Timken roller bearings. The engine and tender have steam brakes which can be worked independently or combined with the vacuum brake system. The box mounted on the tender frame is the right hand feed water sieve which acts as a filter removing dirt and foreign bodies which might otherwise clog the injector. A similar sieve is situated on the left hand side. It had been usual for British locomotives to have a pair of steps below the cab but Bulleid led the way with a single step mounted on the tender, a practice followed by the Riddles team. [L. Elsey]

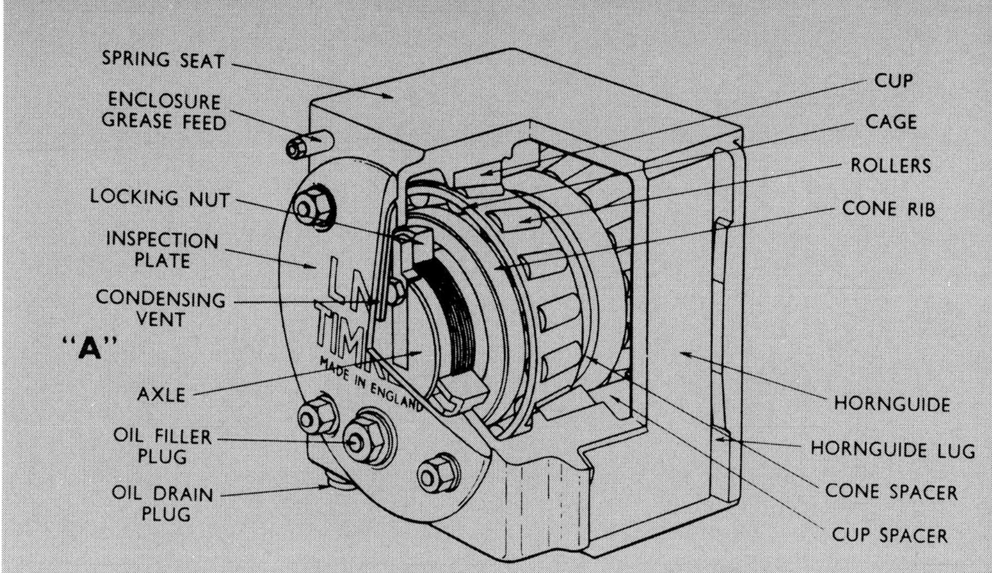

Diagram of tender roller bearing.
[Alan Wills Collection]

The regulator rod of No.73162 shows clearly in this view. Unlike the Pacifics, the Class '5's had a vertical grid sliding regulator valve in the dome, connected to the external rod through the stuffing box mounted on the second ring of the boiler beneath the dome. Immediately in front of the cab on top of the Belpaire firebox is the steam manifold, which could be completely shut off, or each individual cock shut down, restricting the steam flow to the injectors, cab controls and gauges. The modified cab and tender of the later Class '5's may be studied and compared with No.73022 on the opposite page. [M.J. Jackson]

A nicely cleaned No.73022, complete with bowler-hatted Locomotive Inspector on the footplate, blasts away from Wallington on 28 March 1965. Swindon was given prime responsibility for the boiler design and mountings, and generally speaking ex-GWR items were recommended for use on the Standards. However, the GWR design of top feed was not accepted, the Southern type of clack valve being preferred. The two valves, mounted on either side of the boiler's first ring, forced the feed water on two inclined trays which directed the incoming water around the boiler sides away from the tubes. [A.R. Butcher]

73051

A study of No.73051 in action on the Somerset & Dorset section near Midford hauling a Bath to Templecombe local, 1 February 1964. The men who handled Class '5's on this hilly route usually conceded that the Standards had the edge over the original Stanier 4-6-0s, popular though these latter were. [Hugh Ballantyne]

Bath (S. & D.) shed usually maintained its passenger engine allocation in good condition, No.73051 being no exception on 23 March 1964. The research at Swindon into draughting revealed that a small diameter blast pipe and matching chimney proved best for steam raising. However, a narrow stovepipe was not pleasing to British eyes, so the Standards had an outer casing considerably larger than the bore of the internal lining. This casing had a distinctly Lancashire & Yorkshire Railway look about it, but then, E.S. Cox, who was in charge of the design team, grew up at Horwich Works!
[Hugh Ballantyne]

No.73001, minus numberplate and top lamp bracket on the smokebox door, leaves Bath with the 8.45 a.m. excursion to Bournemouth (West) on 30 August 1965. The steam sanders are in action to give the 4-6-0 full adhesion on the steep climb out of the city. [Hugh Ballantyne]

Driver R. Evry of Bath (Green Park) Top Link watches the road ahead as No.73047 heads towards Templcombe with the 9.03 a.m. Bristol to Bournemouth (West) on 13 July 1963. The driver's hand is resting on the reversing wheel, with the pull out regulator handle immediately above and easily within reach. The cut off indicator is on the drum above which are the large and small ejector controls. The vacuum brake valve is the horizontal handle on the pedestal, while above is the steam brake handle. The left-hand water gauge (of GWR origin) and vacuum pressure gauge are also visible. [Hugh Ballantyne]

Contrasting front-ends at Nine Elms shed, 25 February 1967. Rebuilt 'Merchant Navy' No.35013 *Blue Funnel* has a similarly designed running plate and valance to that on Standard Class '5' No.73029, but on the Pacific it was situated at a lower and more traditional height above the coupled wheels. However, it was more difficult to reach the top of the boiler and its mountings from the Bulleid's running plates. [A.R. Butcher]

The Western Section of Southern Region received ten Class '5's, Nos.73110-9, in the mid 1950s. These engines were coupled to BR 1F high capacity tenders, holding 7 tons of fuel and 5625 gallons of water, this latter being extremely useful on the longer runs out of Waterloo. No.73112 was photographed on 18 June 1956, and No.73118 *King Leodegrance* below on 4 March 1960, both at Eastleigh. [L. Elsey]

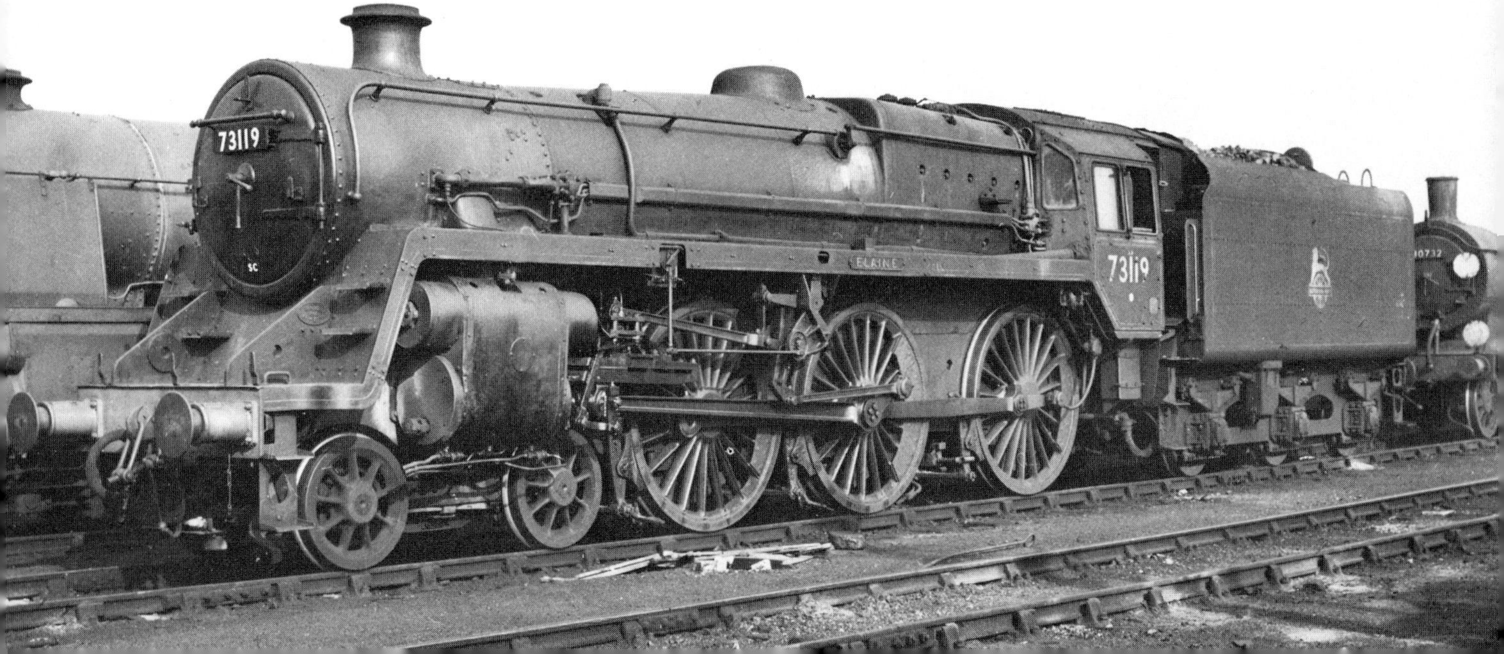

A Scottish-based member of the Class, No.73101, amid sunlight and shadow in Ayr station, with the 5.10 p.m. Glasgow to Stranraer Town on 20 June 1961. This was one of 62 of the class which were coupled to flush-sided tenders holding the usual 7 tons of coal and 4725 gallons of water. Doncaster Drawing Office was responsible for the design of these 4-6-0s and 42 were built in the Plant, but the remainder were constructed at the Derby Works of LM Region. [S. Rickard]

The Class '5's on the Southern replaced withdrawn 'King Arthurs' and Nos. 73080-9 and 73110-9 acquired names originally allocated to the Urie members of the 'N15' Class. Above, No.73117 *Vivien* at Salisbury, 18 April 1964, and below, No.73119 *Elaine* at Eastleigh, 12 October 1959. [A.R. Butcher/L. Elsey]

)ver the years several attempts had been made to introduce Caprotti valve gear on British locomotive lasses. H.G. Ivatt had built a number of Class '5' 4-6-0s with this gear in the final years of the LMSR and it vas decided to use a version of the gear, known as British Caprotti, on Class '8' 4-6-2 No.71000. Because f its success, the final thirty Class '5' 4-6-0s, Nos.73125-154, were so equipped. Rotary cam poppet valves ive excellent steam distribution, allowing for a full expansion of the live steam. Two inlet valves per ylinder are driven by cams actuated by tubular rotating shafts connected to the return crank gearbox vhich is fitted to the driving wheel crank pins. These shafts and gearbox are prominent on No.73126, een at Shrewsbury on 9 August 1956. [Brian Morrison]

A full portrait of No.73126 outside the ex-LMS section of Shrewsbury shed, 9 August 1956. The Caprotti Class '5's were concentrated in 'pockets' around the system, a number being here at Shrewsbury while others were to be found in Scotland, with a few appearing on the St. Pancras trains. They did not often figure in the high speed runs beloved of train-timers, but given the opportunity they could run up to the high 'eighties' with ease, though experienced drivers reckoned that they were weaker on the banks than their Walschaerts sisters. [Brian Morrison]

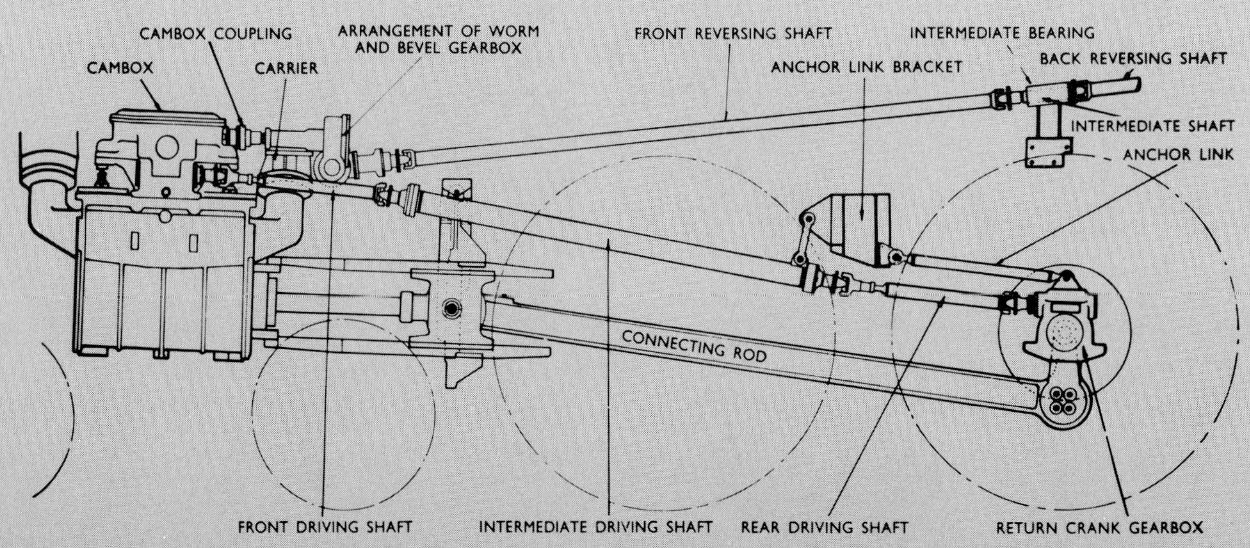

CAMBOX COUPLING
ARRANGEMENT OF WORM AND BEVEL GEARBOX
FRONT REVERSING SHAFT
INTERMEDIATE BEARING
CAMBOX
CARRIER
ANCHOR LINK BRACKET
BACK REVERSING SHAFT
INTERMEDIATE SHAFT
ANCHOR LINK
CONNECTING ROD
FRONT DRIVING SHAFT
INTERMEDIATE DRIVING SHAFT
REAR DRIVING SHAFT
RETURN CRANK GEARBOX

No.73133 at Eastleigh, 5 June 1965. Because of the design of the valve gear, it was not possible to drive the mechanical lubricator pumps in the usual manner, hence the drive from the rear coupled wheel, with both lubricators together under the running plate. [L. Elsey]

The right-hand motion of No.73133 (at Eastleigh, 3 March 1965), showing the worm and bevel gearbox above the front coupled wheel, also the cambox over the steam chest. [L. Elsey]. *Below:* diagram of British Caprotti valve gear. [Alan Wills Collection]

It was decided that certain ex-LMS types were so close to the ideals of the BR design team that, apart from the substitution of Standard details and fittings, they would be entirely suitable to incorporate into the Standard range of Classes. One such was the Class '4' 2-6-0 which was derived from Ivatt's large Mogul, a type which had already been built for service on the Eastern and North Eastern Regions. The LMS engines had been fitted with double chimneys, but the original draughting had not proved satisfactory in service and the 76xxx's carried the normal single blast pipe and chimney. No.76016 is ex-Works at Eastleigh on 2 April 1965. [L. Elsey]

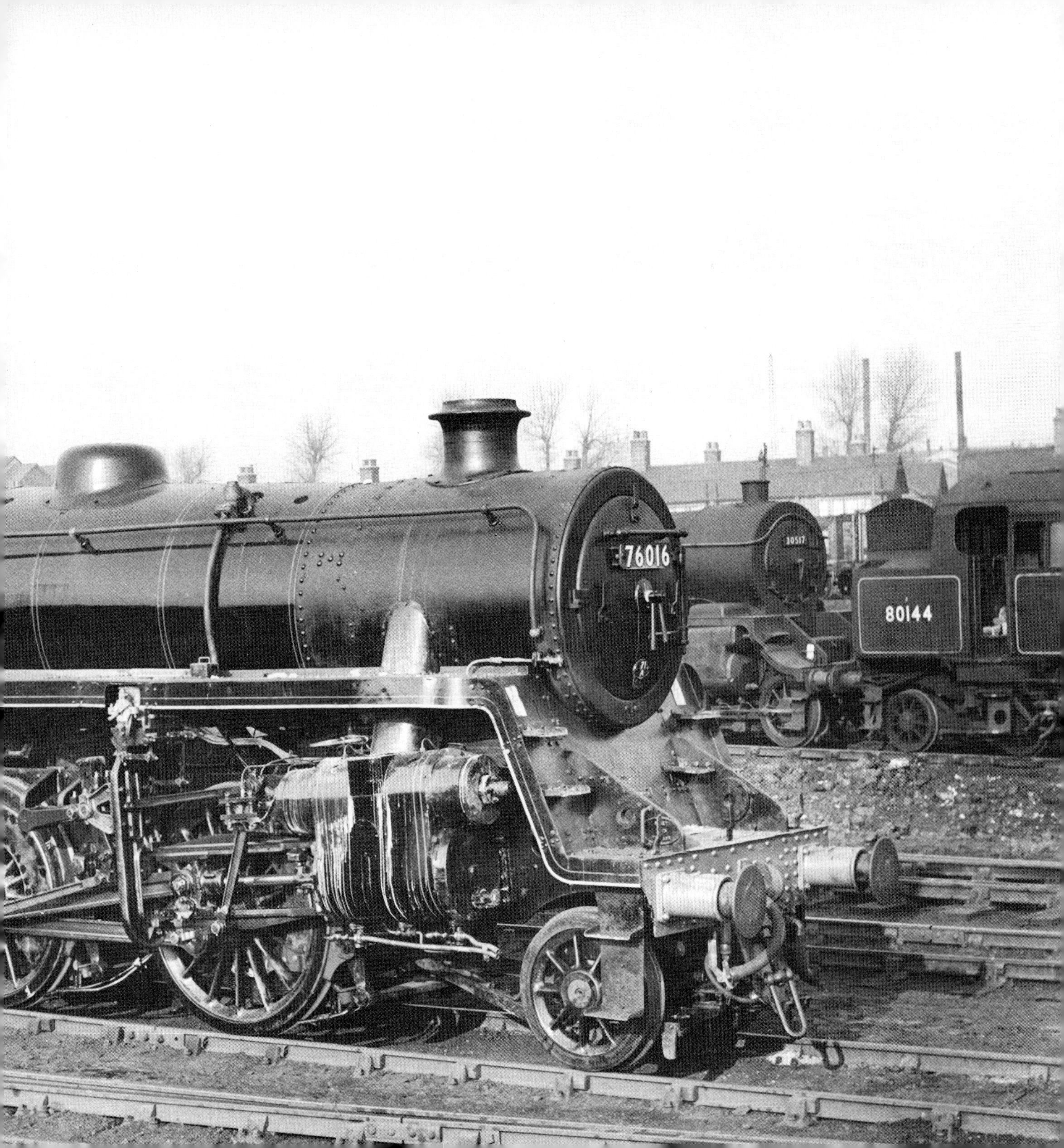
76016
30517
80144

No.76025 at Wimborne with a similar duty, a Brockenhurst to Bournemouth (West) local in April 1964. [Peter Paye]. *Below:* the same locomotive some ten years earlier, outside Eastleigh shed on 2 July 1954. The Ivatt Class '4's were the first British locomotives to have their running platforms fixed so high up on the sides of the boilers and as they had a very shallow valence their appearance seemed most 'un-British'. However, the Standard version had been neatened with a deeper valence and a front fall plate.

[Brian Morrison]

The majority of the Class '4's went to the North of England and Scotland, although the Southern had a small allocation for mixed-traffic duties around Eastleigh and Salisbury. The 5ft.3in. coupled wheels were ideal for freight but the well-designed valve gear and cylinders allowed useful speeds on passenger turns, such as this Weymouth to Eastleigh local, seen at Ringwood with No.76009 as motive power in April 1964.

[Peter Paye]

76025
613

76025
76025

The cylinders (17½in. x 26in.) and motion were almost identical to those of the Ivatt design, with two slide bars, one above and one below the cross head. This arrangement had to be used on the engines having pony trucks as the three-slide design used on the bigger engines did not permit enough clearance between the wheels and slidebars in order to pass the restricted L1 loading gauge. (No.76043, Neasden, 28 November 1954).
[Brian Morrison]

The rear end of No.76018 (Eastleigh, 13 September 1953) showing the footplate floor extension and canvas canopy which was provided to keep the draughts out of the cab. Although much of their work was on freight duties, these Class '4's were fitted with speedometers, the cable of which may be seen connected to the rear coupled wheel. The tender is of the BR 2 type which carried 6 tons of coal, 3500 gallons of water and had a total weight of 42 tons. [L. Elsey]

Another of the S R's Moguls, No.76059, at Eastleigh on 10 October 1960. The plate under the buffer beam protects recently fitted A.W.S. equipment. Doncaster was the parent design office for this class and the building of the 115 locomotives was shared between Horwich, Doncaster and Derby.

[M.J. Jackson]

ourteen of the class, Nos.76053–66, were coupled to the larger BR 1B tenders carrying 7 tons of coal and 4725 gallons of water. These engines were allocated to the Southern Region, where good use was made of this increased fuel capacity. No.76063 stands ready for duty at her home shed, Eastleigh, on 27 November 1956. [L. Elsey]

The B R 1B type tenders suited the Moguls very well, seeming especially so to those used to Southern locomotives, which often were coupled to large water carts. The flush sides of these tenders gave the engines a much less cluttered appearance than some of the Standards. No.76055 has raised steam to full working pressure (225 lbs./sq.in.) at Reading on 21 June 1955. The boiler was almost identical to that of the Ivatt Mogul, having a maximum diameter of 5ft.3in. tapering to 4ft.9in. and with a length of 10ft.10½ins. [Brian Morrison]

No.76069 of Eastleigh (71A) shed leaves Midford (on the Somerset & Dorset line) o 30 May 1959. It will be noticed that the vertical section of the high-sided tender does no match the inward slope of the upper part of the cabside. [Hugh Ballantyne

Detail close-up of No.76019 (Eastleigh, 8 April 1956). The Moguls, like the 4-6-0s already described, had narrow fireboxes, the former having a grate area of 23sq.ft. The cylinder and wheel dimensions allied to the boiler pressure gave a tractive effort of 24,170 lbs. and with the good adhesion factor of 4.65, they were sure-footed and popular performers on moderately loaded freight turns. This particular engine retains the original design of fluted connecting rods. The Class '4's were fitted with plain bearings on all axles, with the exception of Nos.76053-66 which had Timken rollers on their large tenders. [Hugh Ballantyne]

76069

76008
145

The 5ft.3in. Moguls were very much at home on the hillier routes of Britain, including the Southern's West of England main line, where their rapid powers of acceleration proved most useful on through stopping trains; No.76005 is seen heading the 11.05 a.m. Salisbury to Yeovil Junction stopper near Tisbury Gates on 21 August 1958. [Hugh Ballantyne]

No.76008 makes heavy weather of the 7.37 a.m. Bournemouth to Eastleigh stopper as she gets away from Hinton Admiral on 19 August 1966. The 'third rails' for the forthcoming electrification of the line are already partly in place, and the sight and sound of steam in Southern England will soon be but a memory. [W.L. Underhay]

No.76025 on the pits at Eastleigh, 21 October 1956. There is no doubt that such modern engines as the Standards of all classes were much easier to service than older designs, the self-cleaning smokeboxes, drop grates and hopper ash pans all helping to ease the fireman's lot at the end of his shift. Also, of course, there was less preparation for the drivers to perform with such equipment as mechanical lubricators and grease nipples on the mechanical parts. By coincidence, the other engine on the coal road is one of Eastleigh shed's oldest mixed traffic locomotives, 'Jumbo' No.30566 which had been built as long ago as 1885 and had few, if any, concessions to the easing of her crew's daily toil.
[Hugh Ballantyne]

76025

It had been the original intention of the BR authorities to use the Ivatt Class '4' and Class '2' Moguls, the Class '2' 2-6-2T and the Fairburn 2-6-4T more or less as they stood for inclusion in the new Standard range. However, the bigger tank required some modification to allow it to clear the L1 loading gauge. This included the curving inwards of the cabsides, bunker and sidetanks, as may be seen in this view at Christ's Hospital on 13 January 1962, of No.80146 working the 12.19 p.m. Horsham to Brighton stopper. [A.R. Butcher]

Sister engine No.80147 halts adjacent to the old LBSCR water tower at East Grinstead (High Level) and her fireman goes forward to check the sanders after the engine's arduous climb from Forest Row with a London-bound train. This 2-6-4T represents the final flowering of British steam design, but around her is evidence of the strong 'Brighton' influence still clearly visible on the signal box, signal, and water tower, despite the fact that this was recorded as late as June 1960. [C.E. Dann]

Brighton drawing office was made responsible for the design work on the Class '4' tanks and 130 out of the total of 155 in the class were built in Brighton Works. No.80032 entered service in March 1952, was allocated to Brighton (75A) shed and when seen at Eastleigh, a few months later (on 28 August 1952), she was still in splendid external condition. In fact, these tanks were generally considered to be among the

great successes of the Standard range, but then, their pedigree was excellent, descending from the highly successful Fowler tanks through the Stanier and Fairburn developments to the Riddles/Cox concepts of what a modern 2-6-4 mixed-traffic tank should be. [L. Elsey]

80070

No.80070 undergoing an Intermediate Overhaul in the Eastern Region's Stratford Works, 7 July 1956. Published figures relating to that period reveal that the average repair costs per mile for the Class '4' tanks were 7.43d, one of the lowest figures for the whole Standard range. They were running on average over 180,000 miles between General repairs, having an Intermediate about the halfway mark, which would normally be reached after some two years running. [Brian Morrison]

Coal bunkers old and new at Tunbridge Wells shed in May 1959. The veteran is 'H' Class 0-4-4T No.31329, a Wainwright design dating from 1906 while No.80019 was built at Brighton in 1951. The coal capacity of the Class '4' tanks was 3½ tons and the shed staff have crammed every single ounce of that amount into the bunker, a skill which was always much in evidence at the depot. The bogie was similar to that provided for the Class '4' 4-6-0, having 3ft. wheels. [C.E. Dann]

80043
41223
ERCREECH
JUNCTION

No.80012, ex-works at Eastleigh on 9 May 1964. These engines received BR lined-black livery and as few were regularly allocated to Western Region, there were no green-painted members of the class.
[A.R. Butcher]

The water capacity of the Class '4's was 2000 gallons. Unfortunately, while coal can be piled as high as the loading gauge will allow, water cannot be 'trodden in' to the tanks! No.80043 has had more than her fair share of water at Evercreech Junction whilst working the 4.18 p.m. Templecombe to Bath on 7 August 1965.
[Hugh Ballantyne]

Little of the lining shows through the grime covering No.80039, seen working the 9.56 a.m. Okehampton to Padstow at Wadebridge, on 12 June 1964. Like many tank classes, the '4's had ventilation holes in the cab weatherboards. The level recess at the rear corner of the bunker enabled the fireman to climb into the coal space. [Alan Wills]

The Ivatt Class '4' boiler, used for the Standard Mogul and, with modifications, for the Class '4' 4-6-0, was also destined to see service on the Class '4' tank. However, the cylinders were smaller on the Standard tank (18in. x 28in.) compared with those of the Fairburn design (19⅝in. x 26in.) in order to clear the L1 loading gauge, so to make up the tractive effort to the figure of 25,515 lbs. required, the boiler was pressed to 225 lbs./sq.in., with the coupled wheels at 5ft.8in. These dimensions were similar to the specification of the Class '4' 4-6-0 mixed traffic design, but although the main components of the motion of the two types were identical, the tank had two slide bars to support the crosshead, as seen on No.80013 (Redhill, June 1961). [C.E. Dann]

A striking feature from the original LMS design was the oval type of buffer head, the only such on the Standard range. In order to clear the restricted loading gauge, the Standard engines had buffer beams which were inset from the full width of the locomotive. The cylinders, with their 10in. piston valves above, represent the full 8ft.9in. width of the locomotive, with only 7ft.7½in. across the front steps. No.80015 waits quietly in the spring sunshine at Southampton Terminus, 11 May 1965.
[J.R. Besley]

Many fine tank engines have been built at Brighton Works over the years, the final series being the splendid Standard '4's. The local enginemen also appreciated their qualities, which included a free steaming boiler and good accelerative powers. The total weight in full working order is 86½ tons with 53 tons available on the coupled wheels for adhesion (factor 4.65) and the class was widely distributed, proving popular from Cornwall to Scotland. This action photograph shows No.80148 in an area associated with the class from its inception—Groombridge on the Brighton to Tunbridge Wells West route, summer 1960. [Derek Cross]

80148

At least seven members of the class have survived the scrapping holocaust of the 1960s and the first to be fully restored to working order was No.80079 of the Severn Valley Railway. As in their original working days, these big tanks are ideal motive power for stopping trains and should continue to give excellent service to their new owners for many years to come. No.80079 looked particularly smart on 16 April 1977 when she was seen leaving Arley for Foley Park. [J.R. Besley]

With restoration of the mechanical parts well advanced, No.80064 has been decorated for the Queen's Silver Jubilee celebrations, 7 June 1977. The scene is the Dart Valley Railway's workshop at Buckfastleigh, and it is probable that this big Standard will soon be at work on the Company's Torbay and Dartmouth Railway. [J.R. Besley]

The Fairburn 2-6-4Ts and Ivatt Class '2' 2-6-2Ts provided the bases for two sizes of Standard tank engines which could cover most of the branch line and light general duties required of them. However, it was decided that a tank of intermediate power and within a 16½-ton axle loading limit would be a necessary member of the new range of locomotives, hence the 74-ton Class '3' 2-6-2T was designed and built at Swindon Works to a total of 45. Three of these, with No.82025 nearly complete, are under construction in the Factory on the last day of October 1954. The pony trucks on display are of a similar type to those fitted to the bigger Class '4' tanks. [Brian Morrison]

A pair of newly-constructed Class '3's, Nos.82001/2, outside the shed at Stratford-on-Avon, 22 June 1952. In those days it was the usual practice to remove the steam-heat hoses for storage during the summer months; the connection for these may be seen below the buffer beams. [T.E. Williams]

No.82036 takes water (from a split hosepipe) at Nailsworth, 21 June 1963. The tanks had a water capacity of 1500 gallons.
[A.R. Butcher]

A number of the Class '3' tanks went new to South Wales to provide modern motive power on the difficult passenger duties which had to be performed on the hilly valley routes. Originally these tanks, like the larger Class '4's, were painted in BR mixed-traffic black livery, but many of Western Region's allocation were given lined green livery in the late 1950s. No.82043 is fully coaled and ready for work on shed at Barry, 19 July 1955. [S. Rickard]

No.82039 barks away from Shepton Mallet with the lightly-loaded 3.28 p.m. Witham to Yatton on 27 July 1963. The Class '3' had a tractive effort of 21,490 lbs., a useful figure for a branch line tank engine and combined with the adhesion factor of 5.08 gave good accelerative powers. [Hugh Ballantyne]

It had been hoped to use the Ivatt Class '4' boiler on the two Class '3' designs, but this would have been too heavy for the 16-ton axle loading aimed at, so it was decided to adapt the very successful GWR No.2 boiler which had been used on such classes as the '51xx', '81xx' and '56xx' tanks. By using the Swindon flanging plates, giving diameters of 4ft.5in. to 5ft.0½in. the boiler was in basic respects of Churchward design, but shortened by almost 6 inches to fit the

new chassis of the Class '3'. Of course, the original design was domeless, but in order to allow the fitting of such standardised components as the regulator and top feed, a dome was provided and the usual Standard clack valves were placed astride the front ring of the boiler, which was pressed to 200 lb./sq.in. No.82014 is posed for her portrait at Eastleigh on 4 October 1952. [L. Elsey]

No.82005, in Brunswick green livery, on shed at Machynlleth, 11 September 1963. She has been coaled up with three tons of best quality fuel, this capacity giving the class a reasonable radius of action. For a modern design, the cab spectacles are on the small side, as this view shows. As with the other smaller Standard types, the Class '3's had a pair of live steam injectors mounted below the fireman's side of the cab. [Lawrence Waters]

No.82043, of Bath Road shed, passes Kilver Street crossing at Shepton Mallet, with the 2.52 p.m. Yatton to Witham on 23 May 1959. It will be noticed that these engines (in common with the smaller Class '2') had straight-sided tanks and cabs instead of the 'slope-in' of the other designs. The overall width of the water tanks is 8ft.6in., sufficiently narrow to clear the L1 loading gauge, but these high-topped tanks gave the crew poor forward visibility, which did little to enhance their already slender popularity. Prominent on these Class '3' engines are the metal plates shielding the lubricators mounted on the running plates alongside the smokebox.
[Hugh Ballantyne]

No.82036 pulls away from Dinas Powis, in the Cardiff Valleys Division, with the 11.00 a.m. Barry Island to Merthyr in September 1955. The aforementioned poor visibility when running forward is in evidence, the driver having to lean out of the side window. On Western Region this was to prove an even greater handicap for the drivers who were normally used to sighting their signals from the traditional right-hand side of Great Western cabs. [S. Rickard]

The Class '3' tanks were in line with the Class '4' 2-6-0s already described, having 5ft.3in. coupled wheels (as did the similar Class '3' Moguls). The cast-steel cylinders, with cast-iron liners, measured 17½in.x26in. and were served by 10in. piston valves actuated by the easily accessible Walschaerts valve gear. As with all the Standard classes, the valves were of the long-travel type, moving $6\frac{7}{16}$in. in full forward gear (75 per cent) with a steam lap of 1½in. and a lead of ¼in. The motion is very similar to that of the larger Class '4' tanks, and the reversing gear is of the same design. All the Standards had a considerable amount of pipe-work hidden beneath the running plates and some of this is visible below the water tank of No.82040 (Exmouth Junction shed, 8 March 1965). [J.R. Besley]

No.82034 in the typically Great Western setting of Bovey Tracey with the 5.15 p.m. Mortonhampstead to Newton Abbot on 14 August 1956. Although a small engine, the Class '3' tank had all the refinements accorded to modern classes, such as a self-cleaning smokebox, hopper ash pan and rocking grate. Yet in spite of these and other features, they were not popular engines, particularly on the Western where the men were far happier with their old 45xx's. Much of this was probably ingrained prejudice, but it is true to say that these Standards did not sparkle and on the road were little in advance of similarly-sized machines of earlier vintage.
[Hugh Ballantyne]

82034

A bunker-first view of a Standard Class '3' at the head of a Treherbert to Barry Island train near Maesmawr, south of Pontypridd, on 13 October 1956. In retrospect, the building of 45 Class '3's was unnecessary as there was little or no real work for them to do. Already there were signs of impending closures and dieselisation when the class first appeared in 1952 and before long they were working alongside Class '2' tanks, while the heavier duties were performed by the competent Class '4's. So the Class '3's remained as the 'in-betweens' of the BR Standard range.
[S. Rickard]

MIDLAND
OF THE BORDER
NORTH EASTERN
STEAM
GREAT WESTERN
STEAM MISCELLANY
BODMIN AND WADEBRIDGE
STANDARD STEAM
IN ACTION
BRITISH
NARROW GAUG
STEAM
A PICTORIAL SURV
GREAT WESTERN
BRANCH LINE STEAM 2
DIESELS
ON SCOTTISH REGION
BR DIESELS
IN THE
LANDSCA
BR DIESELS
IN ACTION
BRITISH
MOTIVES
H. C. CASSERLEY
IRISH RAILWAYS
in the heyday of steam
OPEAN
TEAM
ERN
MOTIVE
SOUTHERN 188
THE LYNTON & BARNSTAPLE RAILWAY
THE WARSHIPS
THE WAINWRIGHT
ASSES
STEAM
NORTH EASTERN
STEAM
IN ACTION
LONDON MIDLAND
STEAM IN ACTION 4
42/43 DIESEL-HYDRAULICS
LONDON
RT
BUS
UTHERN
AROUND BRIT
8F
GREAT
CENTRAL
recalled